# Learn to Draw
# Enchanted Forest

www.av2books.com

AV² provides enriched content that supplements and complements this book. Weigl's AV² books strive to create inspired learning and engage young minds in a total learning experience.

## Your AV² Media Enhanced books come alive with...

**Audio**
Listen to sections of the book read aloud.

**Key Words**
Study vocabulary, and complete a matching word activity.

**Video**
Watch informative video clips.

**Quizzes**
Test your knowledge.

**Embedded Weblinks**
Gain additional information for research.

**Slide Show**
View images and captions, and prepare a presentation.

**Try This!**
Complete activities and hands-on experiments.

**... and much, much more!**

Go to **www.av2books.com**, and enter this book's unique code.

## BOOK CODE

**C 8 2 1 9 4 9**

**AV² by Weigl** brings you media enhanced books that support active learning.

Published by AV² by Weigl
350 5ᵗʰ Avenue, 59ᵗʰ Floor
New York, NY 10118
Website: www.weigl.com    www.av2books.com

Library of Congress Cataloging-in-Publication Data

Pratt, Laura.
 Enchanted forest / Laura Pratt.
   pages cm. --  (Learn to draw)
 ISBN 978-1-62127-336-3 (hardcover : alk. paper) -- ISBN 978-1-62127-340-0 (softcover : alk. paper)
 1.  Fantasy in art--Juvenile literature. 2.  Drawing--Technique--Juvenile literature.  I. Title.
 NC825.F25P73 2013
 743'.87--dc23
                         2012041029

Printed in the United States of America in North Mankato, Minnesota
1 2 3 4 5 6 7 8 9 0   17 16 15 14 13

052013
WEP040413

Senior Editor: Heather Kissock
Art Director: Terry Paulhus

Every reasonable effort has been made to trace ownership and to obtain permission to reprint copyright material. The publishers would be pleased to have any errors or omissions brought to their attention so that they may be corrected in subsequent printings.

Weigl acknowledges Getty Images as its primary image supplier for this title.

# Contents

# Why Draw?

**D**rawing is easier than you think. Look around you. The world is made of shapes and lines. By combining simple shapes and lines, anything can be drawn. An orange is just a circle with a few details added. A flower can be a circle with ovals drawn around it. An ice cream cone can be a triangle topped with a circle. Most anything, no matter how complicated, can be broken down into simple shapes.

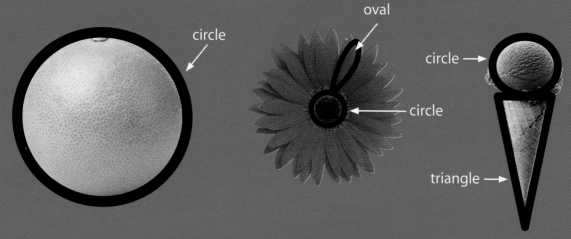

circle

oval

circle →

circle

triangle →

Drawing helps people make sense of the world. It is a way to reduce an object to its simplest form, say our most personal feelings and thoughts, or show others objects from our **imagination**. Drawing an object can help you learn how it fits together and works.

**What shapes do you see in this car?**

It is fun to put the world onto a page, but it is also a good way to learn. Learning to draw even simple objects introduces the skills needed to fully express oneself visually. Drawing is an excellent form of **communication** and improves people's imagination.

Practice drawing your favorite enchanted creature in this book to learn the basic skills necessary to draw. You can use those skills to create your own drawings.

# Enchanted Forest

An enchanted forest is not a real place. It is a place made up of **characters** and creatures from fairy tales and ancient **folktales**. For centuries, storytellers have set their tales in this magical landscape because of the endless adventures that can unfold there.

An enchanted forest is a place of magic and fantasy. It is where fairies live, along with unicorns, gnomes, trolls, and all manner of monsters. Anything can happen in these charmed locations and does. Horses can fly, wolves can carry princesses on their backs, and birds can share secrets with humans. It is a wonderful land of make-believe.

As you draw the creatures in this book, think about what it would be like to live in a land of enchantment. Think about the type of magic you would possess and what you would do with it.

# What Is a Fairy?

A fairy looks much like a tiny version of a human being and is usually female. While fairies are generally thought to be helpful creatures, they were originally depicted as mischievous and mean. In some ancient **cultures**, people believed fairies kidnapped babies and bit people. However, one thing a fairy could never do was tell a lie.

Fairies were introduced in **legends** and folklore many centuries ago. They play key roles in fairy tales such as *Sleeping Beauty* and *Cinderella*. One of the best-known fairies is Tinkerbell. She is a character in the story of *Peter Pan*.

## Fairy Dust

Fairies are believed to have magical powers. Many fairies perform their magic using fairy dust. Fairy dust is kept in a pouch that hangs around their neck or from a belt at their waist.

**Hair**
Fairies are most often portrayed having blond hair. However, in some stories, fairies have black, red, or brown hair as well. As fairies are creatures of the forest, they usually decorate their hair with wildflowers.

**Eyes and Ears**
Some stories say that fairies have green eyes. Sometimes, fairies are portrayed with pointed ears as well.

**Wings**
Fairies get from one place to another by flying. Some fairies have insect-like wings on their back. Other fairies are said to use magical powers to fly.

**Clothing**
Fairy clothing is often light and fluttery. Some fairies are portrayed wearing long gowns. Others are described as wearing short dresses. Many cultures believe fairies like to wear green because of their love of nature.

# How to Draw a Fairy

1. Start with a simple stick figure of the fairy. Use ovals for the head and body, and lines for the arms and legs.

2. Now, draw the body ovals to make the fairy's arms and legs.

**3** Next, draw the face, and outline the fairy's clothing.

**4** Next, draw outlines for her hair, hands, and feet.

**5** In this step, draw the outline for the fairy's wings.

**6** Next, draw the jewelry, and add details to the clothing and wings.

**7** Add finer details to the face, hair, and clothing.

**8** Erase the extra lines and the stick figure.

**9** Color the image.

# What Is a Dragon?

Fire-breathing dragons are some of the largest creatures found in the enchanted forest. A dragon usually looks like a long, scaly lizard. The term *dragon* comes from the Greek word "drakon," which means serpent or snake.

Dragons have appeared in the legends and **myths** of almost every culture in the world. In some European myths, the dragon is a symbol of evil. Often, a knight in a European tale makes it his mission to slay a dragon in order to rescue a princess. In Chinese culture, the dragon is thought of much differently. Chinese dragons are a symbol of power and luck.

## Wings

Not all dragons have wings, but almost all dragons can fly. Many dragons have large wings that look like those of a bat.

## Fire

Many dragons are feared for their ability to breathe fire. Hot flames bursting from the dragon's mouth can be a deadly weapon. One such fire-breathing monster comes from Greek mythology. The Chimera breathed fire like a dragon but had the body of a lion in the front, a goat in the middle, and a snake at the tail.

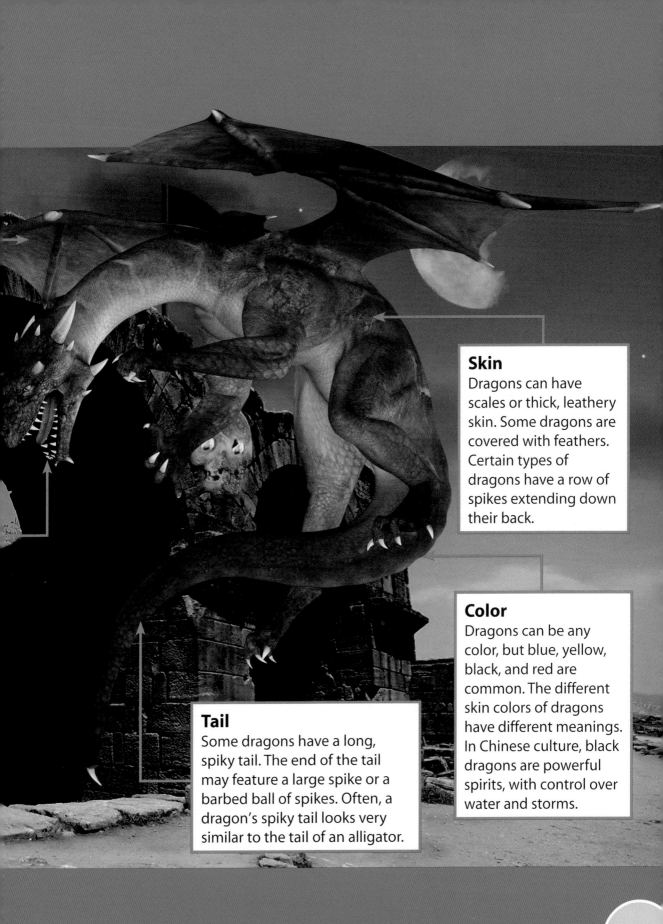

## Skin
Dragons can have scales or thick, leathery skin. Some dragons are covered with feathers. Certain types of dragons have a row of spikes extending down their back.

## Color
Dragons can be any color, but blue, yellow, black, and red are common. The different skin colors of dragons have different meanings. In Chinese culture, black dragons are powerful spirits, with control over water and storms.

## Tail
Some dragons have a long, spiky tail. The end of the tail may feature a large spike or a barbed ball of spikes. Often, a dragon's spiky tail looks very similar to the tail of an alligator.

# How to Draw a Dragon

**1** Start by drawing stick figures for the dragon. Use ovals for the head and body, and lines for the legs and tail.

**2** Draw curved lines around the body ovals to form the head, legs, and tail.

**3** Next, draw the dragon's feet and face.

**4** Next, draw its wings.

**5** In this step, draw the dragon's teeth, horns, and claws.

**6** Next, add finer details to the head and wings.

**7** Add more details to the wings and body.

**8** Erase the extra lines and the stick figure.

**9** Color the image.

# What Is a Gnome?

Gnomes are creatures that are believed to live underground. Like fairies, they are similar to humans in appearance. Gnomes are much shorter than humans. A typical gnome is said to have a height of about 6 inches (15 centimeters).

The origin of gnomes is unknown. Some think gnomes were first part of **Scandinavian** folklore, but most European countries have stories about gnome-like creatures. These stories tell of the gnome's ability to protect and heal the animals in the forest. They also refer to the long lives of gnomes. Some gnomes are believed to have lived for more than 400 years.

## Hat

Female gnomes are usually shown wearing a green cap on their head. This allows them to blend in with the nature around them. Male gnomes are known for their red, pointed caps.

## Eyes

Most gnomes are portrayed with gray eyes. They are known for their deep, penetrating stare.

## Beard

Most male gnomes are shown with long, gray beards. They may or may not have a matching mustache.

## Arms and Legs

Gnomes are known for their strength. Stories tell of them outrunning animals and lifting seven times the weight that a human can.

## Clothing

Male gnomes are said to wear colorful clothing. They are often portrayed wearing a blue shirt and brown pants. A tool belt normally sits around their waist. Female gnomes prefer to wear clothes that allow them to blend in with their environment. They normally are portrayed wearing long skirts and long-sleeved blouses.

# How to Draw a Gnome

**1** Start by drawing a simple stick figure of the gnome. Use ovals for the head and body, and lines for the legs and arms.

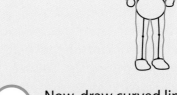

**2** Now, draw curved lines around the body ovals for the arms and legs.

**3** Draw outlines for the eyes and beard.

**4** Next, draw the gnome's hands, feet, and clothing.

**5** In this step, draw the gnome's hat, hands, and belt.

**6** Next, add details to the face and boots.

**7** Add details to the beard, hair, and feet.

**8** Erase the extra lines.

**9** Color the image.

# What Is a Magical Tree?

Trees play an extremely important role in an enchanted forest. They provide **canopy** and protection from harsh conditions such as rain and snow. Trees are also a source of fear. They can shelter all kinds of scary things within their dark leafy undergrowth.

In some cases, the trees of the forest are themselves enchanted. They can talk and move their branches. Sometimes, trees use their branches to push people a certain way. They have also been known to uproot themselves to chase after anyone who comes too close.

**Trunk**
Trees are among the oldest living **organisms** on the planet. Their trunks are gnarled and lumpy. If people look closely enough, they may see a human-like face within the tree trunk. Knots within the trunk open to become eyes. A large hole becomes the tree's mouth.

## Branches

The trees in the enchanted forest have twisted branches that work like arms and fingers. They can reach out and grab objects or push them away.

## Roots

A magical tree is able to lift its roots out of the ground. When this happens, the roots act as the tree's legs. The tree can then run after people or simply move to a better spot. Sometimes, the roots are used to curl around people to trap them.

# How to Draw a Magical Tree

**1** Start with a simple stick figure of the magical tree. Use curved lines for the trunk and branches.

**2** Draw outlines for the trunk and branches.

**3** Next, draw a face on the trunk.

**4** Next, draw ovals for the fruit.

**5** In this step, detail the branches.

**6** Next, draw the roots, and add details to the face and branches.

**7** Add more details to the trunk and roots.

**8** Erase the extra lines.

**9** Color the image.

# What Is a Troll?

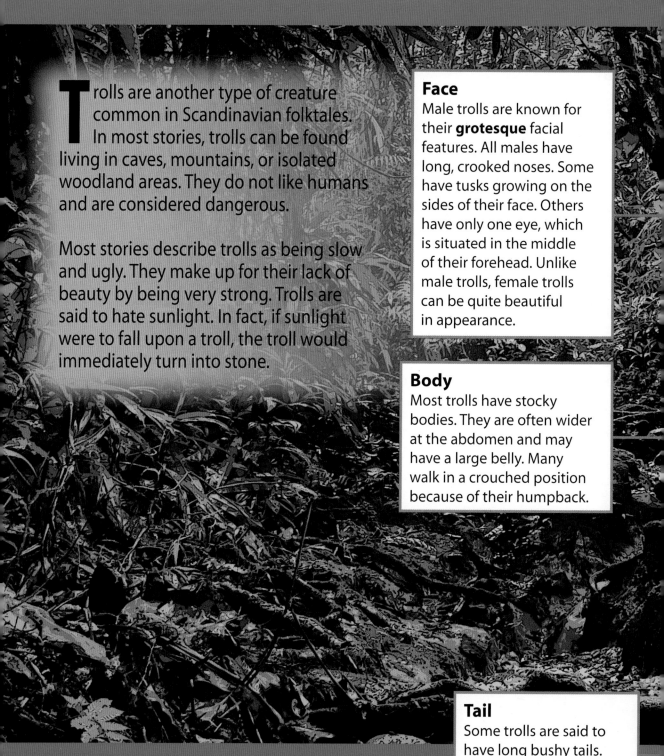

Trolls are another type of creature common in Scandinavian folktales. In most stories, trolls can be found living in caves, mountains, or isolated woodland areas. They do not like humans and are considered dangerous.

Most stories describe trolls as being slow and ugly. They make up for their lack of beauty by being very strong. Trolls are said to hate sunlight. In fact, if sunlight were to fall upon a troll, the troll would immediately turn into stone.

## Face
Male trolls are known for their **grotesque** facial features. All males have long, crooked noses. Some have tusks growing on the sides of their face. Others have only one eye, which is situated in the middle of their forehead. Unlike male trolls, female trolls can be quite beautiful in appearance.

## Body
Most trolls have stocky bodies. They are often wider at the abdomen and may have a large belly. Many walk in a crouched position because of their humpback.

## Tail
Some trolls are said to have long bushy tails. They often hide their tail in their clothing.

**Hair**
Trolls are very hairy. Their hair is quite shaggy and difficult to comb. Some trolls have moss growing on their face instead of hair.

**Fingers and Toes**
A troll has very long arms that can extend almost to the ground. Trolls have only four fingers and four toes on each limb.

# How to Draw a
# Troll

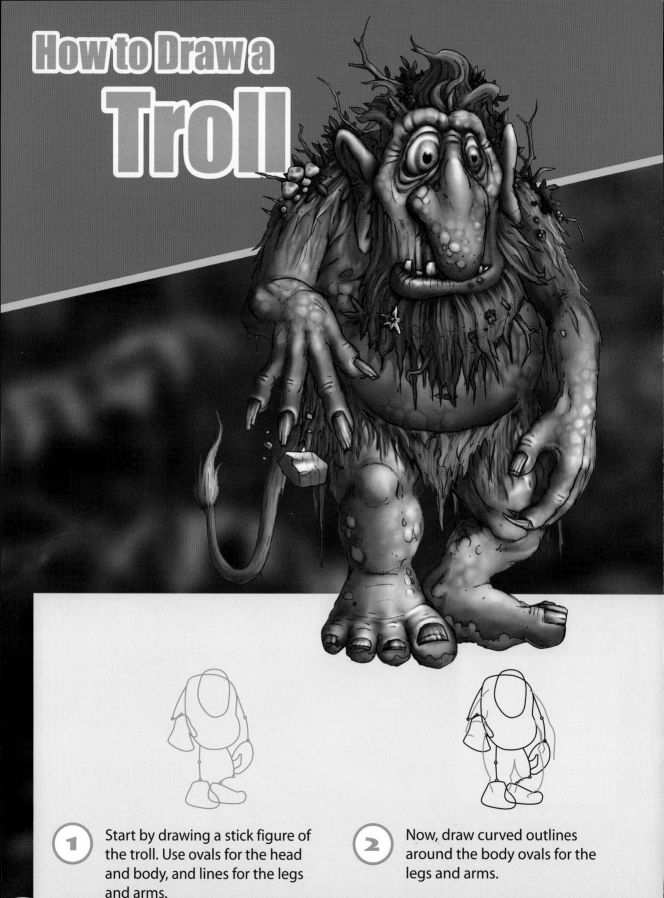

1. Start by drawing a stick figure of the troll. Use ovals for the head and body, and lines for the legs and arms.

2. Now, draw curved outlines around the body ovals for the legs and arms.

**3** Next, draw the outline for troll's face.

**4** Next, draw the outline for the troll's hair, fingers, and toes.

**5** In this step, draw the troll's tail and clothing.

**6** Next, draw its fingernails. Add details to the face, beard, and toes.

**7** Add more details to the hair, face, body, fingers, and toes.

**8** Erase the extra lines.

**9** Color the Image.

# What Is a Unicorn?

A unicorn is much like a horse but with one unique feature, its horn. Unicorns live in enchanted forests but are hard to catch. They swiftly run away from any hunter who tries to capture them. Only a **maiden** who is **pure** in heart can hope to tame a unicorn.

Many ancient texts refer to the unicorn. These works, including the Old Testament of the Bible, discuss the unicorn as if it really existed. Today, the unicorn is only a creature of legends. It is thought to be a symbol of purity and grace.

## Horn

A unicorn's most remarkable feature is its horn. The horn grows out of the unicorn's forehead. It is usually shown as straight with a spiral groove. In ancient times, people believed that the unicorn's horn had **supernatural** powers. They thought that if the horn were crushed into a powder, that powder could work magic. According to some legends, the powder could turn poison into harmless water and cure many diseases.

**Body**
A unicorn's body looks like that of a beautiful horse. Unicorns are almost always white. Besides their long white manes, some unicorns are also said to have a beard similar to that of a goat.

**Hoofs**
Some unicorns have goat's hoofs. They are cloven, which means they have two parts. A horse's hoofs, on the other hand, have only one part.

**Tail**
Most unicorns are pictured with a long, white horse's tail. Some, however, are drawn with a tail similar to that of a lion.

# How to Draw a Unicorn

**1** Start by drawing a simple stick figure for the unicorn. Use ovals for the head and body, and lines for the legs.

**2** Draw curved lines around the body ovals for the legs and head.

**3** Next, draw the unicorn's mane and ear.

**4** Next, draw the outline for the tail.

**5** Draw the outline for the horn.

**6** Next, draw outlines for the hoofs.

**7** Add details to the mane and tail.

**8** Erase the extra lines and the stick figure.

**9** Color the image.

# Test Your Knowledge of Enchanted Forests

## 1.

Name two fairy tales that feature fairies.

*Answer: Sleeping Beauty and Cinderella*

## 2.

What animal does a dragon look like?

Answer: A lizard

## 3.

Where are gnomes believed to live?

Answer: Underground

## 4.

Which parts of a tree in the enchanted forest may form its face?

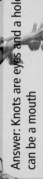

Answer: Knots are eyes and a hole can be a mouth

## 5.

What happens to a troll if sunlight falls upon it?

Answer: It turns into stone

## 6.

What traits or qualities does the unicorn represent?

Answer: Purity and grace

Want to learn more? Log on to av2books.com to access more content.

# Draw an Environment

## Materials
- Large white poster board
- Internet connection or library
- Pencils and crayons or markers
- Glue or tape

## Steps
1. Complete one of the drawings in this book. Cut out the drawing.
2. Using this book, the internet, and a library, find out more about the enchanted character you have drawn.
3. Think about where your character lives. What type of environment surrounds the character? What features does the area have? Are there other people or characters? What do they look like?
4. On a large white poster board, draw an environment for your character. Be sure to place all the features you noted in step 3.
5. Place the cutout drawing in its environment with glue or tape. Color the drawing's environment to complete the activity.

# Key Words

**canopy:** the uppermost part of a forest, which provides cover and blocks light from smaller trees and plants

**characters:** people and creatures portrayed in a work of fiction

**communication:** the sending and receiving of information

**cultures:** particular groups of people at specific points in time

**folktales:** a collection of traditional beliefs and stories by a specific culture

**grotesque:** strangely distorted

**imagination:** the ability to form new creative ideas or images

**legends:** unverified stories handed down from earlier times, usually believed to be based on history

**maiden:** a young, unmarried woman

**myths:** ancient stories dealing with supernatural beings and heroes

**organisms:** all living things

**pure:** free from sin or guilt; innocent

**Scandinavian:** relating to people from Norway, Finland, Sweden, Iceland, and Denmark

**supernatural:** a power that seems to go beyond natural forces

# Log on to www.av2books.com

AV² by Weigl brings you media enhanced books that support active learning. Go to www.av2books.com, and enter the special code found on page 2 of this book. You will gain access to enriched and enhanced content that supplements and complements this book. Content includes video, audio, weblinks, quizzes, a slide show, and activities.

## AV² Online Navigation

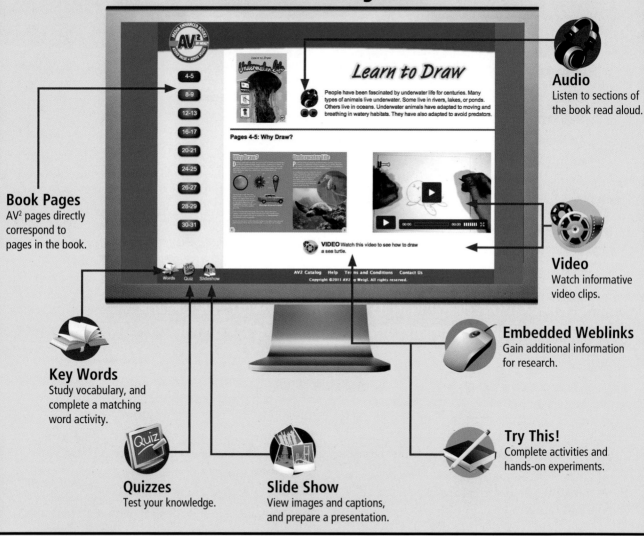

**Book Pages**
AV² pages directly correspond to pages in the book.

**Audio**
Listen to sections of the book read aloud.

**Video**
Watch informative video clips.

**Key Words**
Study vocabulary, and complete a matching word activity.

**Quizzes**
Test your knowledge.

**Slide Show**
View images and captions, and prepare a presentation.

**Embedded Weblinks**
Gain additional information for research.

**Try This!**
Complete activities and hands-on experiments.

---

AV² was built to bridge the gap between print and digital. We encourage you to tell us what you like and what you want to see in the future.

## Sign up to be an AV² Ambassador at www.av2books.com/ambassador.